CHRISTIE'S
COLLECTIBLES

CHRISTIE'S
COLLECTIBLES

TEAPOTS

Paul Tippett

A BULFINCH PRESS BOOK
LITTLE, BROWN AND COMPANY
BOSTON • NEW YORK • TORONTO • LONDON

Copyright © 1996 by Marshall Editions Developments Limited

All rights reserved.
No part of this publication may be reproduced
in any form or by any electronic
or mechanical means, including information storage and
retrieval systems, without permission in writing from the publisher,
except by a reviewer who may quote
brief passages in a review.

First North American Edition

ISBN 0-8212-2269-4

Library of Congress Catalog Card Number 95-80527

EDITOR GWEN RIGBY
DESIGNER HELEN SPENCER
PICTURE EDITOR ELIZABETH LOVING

Marshall Editions would like to thank
Edward Schneider of Christie's Images for his help
in the creation of this book.

Conceived, edited, and designed by
Marshall Editions
170 Piccadilly London W1V 9DD

Bulfinch Press is an imprint and trademark of
Little, Brown and Company (Inc.)

Published simultaneously in Canada by
Little, Brown & Company (Canada) Limited

PRINTED IN PORTUGAL

CHRISTIE'S
502 Park Avenue New York NY 10022

CHRISTIE'S EAST
219 East 67th Street New York NY 10021

CHRISTIE'S CANADA
170 Bloor Street West Suite 210 Toronto Ontario M5S IT9

CHRISTIE'S
8 King Street St. James's London SW1Y 6QT

CHRISTIE'S SOUTH KENSINGTON
85 Old Brompton Road London SW7 3LD

CHRISTIE'S AUSTRALIA
298 New South Head Road Double Bay Sydney NSW 2028

CHRISTIE'S SOUTH AFRICA
P.O. Box 72126 Parkview Johannesburg 2122

CHRISTIE'S JAPAN
Sankyo Ginza Building 6-5-13 Ginza Chuo-ku Tokyo 104

Contents

INTRODUCTION 6
CHINESE 12
JAPANESE 18
FAIENCE 22
MEISSEN 24
VIENNA 26
VENICE 27
LATER MEISSEN 28
FRENCH 18TH CENTURY 32
GERMAN 18TH CENTURY 35
ENGLISH 18TH CENTURY 36
ENGLISH IMARI 54
ENGLISH 19TH CENTURY 56

SÈVRES 58
PARIS 59
GERMAN & AUSTRIAN
    20TH CENTURY 60
AESTHETIC MOVEMENT 64
ART NOUVEAU 65
BELLEEK 66
MINTON 67
WEMYSS WARE 68
BARGE STYLE 69
ENGLISH 20TH CENTURY 70
GLOSSARY & INDEX 78
ACKNOWLEDGMENTS 80

PRICE CODES
The following price codes are used in this book:
$A Less than $150 **$B** $151–$750
$C $751–$1,500 **$D** $1,501–$3,000 **$E** $3,001–$7,500
$F $7,501–$15,000 **$G** More than $15,000

Valuation is an imprecise art and prices can vary for many
reasons, including the condition of a piece, fashion, and national and
regional interest. Prices given in this book are approximate
and based on likely *auction* values. *Insurance* values reflect the
retail replacement price and as such are liable to be higher.

Introduction

*T*EA DRINKING ORIGINATED IN CHINA, THE HOME OF THE tea plant, which is a relative of the camellia. No one is sure precisely when the Chinese began to pick and brew the fragrant leaves of the tea plant, but the habit was well established prior to the Han period (206 B.C.–220 A.D.). Tea – which was prepared either from dried green leaves or from roasted black leaves – was relished as a stimulant to scholastic and meditative activities and, as such, soon secured a respected place in society.

*I*nitially exclusive to the elevated and educated classes, tea drinking gradually became accessible to all. Specific rituals and implements were soon associated with this

This rice-paper painting, dating from c.1820, shows tea being packed for export in a warehouse near the waterfront at Canton.

Tea drinking had already become a bourgeois custom when the Flemish artist J.J. Horemans painted this c.1740.

respected drink. The teapot probably derived from the ceramic kettles and wine pots with shaped spouts and bail (overhead) handles, which were originally made in bronze and other metals and had been a feature of Chinese cultural life for thousands of years. As befitted a drink that was made from precious leaves, then drunk in tiny bowls, teapots tended to be smaller than the wine pots they resembled.

For much of its history, China was significantly more advanced than Europe – indeed, the Chinese were proficient potters and had mastered the difficult art of making porcelain at least 2,000 years before the Europeans did so. It also produced many other luxury goods which were in great demand internationally. And, since trade in goods leads to the exchange of cultural habits, tea drinking spread initially to the Asian nations that had had the longest association with China. But

A scene of European merchants unloading cargoes at a wharf, painted on Meissen porcelain c.1730.

China was a strongly centralized and closed society, so any potential trading partner had to seek a special agreement. Trade by sea was established by the Arabs in the 6th and 7th centuries A.D.; the Portuguese were the first Europeans to reach the country in any number, in the 16th century. Others followed, and the Chinese controlled the traffic with these nations by directing them out of restricted areas, principally to Canton, which became the focus for most trade with the Europeans – British, Dutch, and French among them.

*A*n obsession developed in Europe with all things Chinese, and from the end of the 17th century, tea was shipped from China as part of the export of exotic spices and luxury goods, such as silks, gold, lacquer, and fans. China's ability to supply tea, and the craze in the West for drinking it, was such that it soon became the major cargo, and from the 1720s tea filled about 90 percent of the space in ships' holds. The ships that brought the tea also carried the porcelain teapots, tea bowls, and saucers that were deemed to be essential to the sophisticated enjoyment of tea drinking. But it was initially the preserve of the upper classes, since only they were able to afford to buy tea, which was immensely expensive, and the Chinese vessels to serve it in – particularly desirable since porcelain could not be produced in Europe at that time.

Although European potters had long sought to imitate Chinese porcelain, which was regarded as far superior to the native pottery, they had met with little success, and for a long time tin-glazed wares (also known as faience or delft) were the closest in terms of a fine white glazed ware that they could produce. It was, therefore, quite logical that when Europeans began to make their own tea wares they looked to Chinese and Japanese porcelain models for the source of inspiration for their own designs.

The harbor front at Canton in 1820; most of the tea exported from China passed through this port.

The Chinese had explored many forms and techniques in the manufacture of teapots well before their wares reached the West. European potters took on both these traditions and a vocabulary of decoration from China and Japan that could have had little meaning for them apart from their decorative and exotic appeal. They built on these traditions and, in turn, developed their own ideas of what constituted a good teapot and how it should be decorated.

As a result, the teapot is an extremely interesting and rewarding subject for the collector. For enshrined within an object that today is generally viewed as ordinary and commonplace are countless cross-cultural references and thousands of years of tradition.

Chinese ladies are pictured drinking tea in this rice-paper painting dating from c.1820.

The first Chinese teapots exported were painted in blue and white, and European potters copied both colors and designs.

TIPS FOR COLLECTORS

• Most people start by buying an object they like or which interests them, then they pick up a few more, and, before they know it, they have begun a collection.

• Theme the collection. Specialize in a particular area, for instance: within a date range; a particular type, such as blue and white printed teapots; on a geographical basis – just English teapots or Chinese ones.

• Decide how much you can spend. Remember that damaged items are always cheaper than perfect ones. Sell items that do not fit in with your theme to buy those that do.

• Learn about your subject. Join collector's groups; seek out dealers and auctions that sell the items you are interested in; go to museums and exhibitions; and read about the subject.

Chinese Yixing

THE MOST COMMON FORM OF CHINESE TEAPOT
is the Yixing ("ee-ching") teapot made of a red clay.
These pottery wares take their name from the Yixing
kilns in eastern China and are usually unglazed,
giving them a matte appearance.

TEAPOTS OF THIS TYPE, WHICH WERE AMONG THE
first imported into Europe, were some of
the earliest to be imitated, so it is easy for collectors
to confuse good-quality European versions
with the Chinese originals.

BOTH THE TEAPOTS SHOWN HERE DEMONSTRATE
strong traditional Chinese decoration. The globular
teapot (top), with its design inspired by the natural
forms much favored at the Yixing kilns, is a
model frequently copied
in Europe during
the 18th century.

Height 5½in/14cm $B

THE PHOENIX SHAPE
(right) is unusual and
dates from the 1600s.

Length 6½in/16.5cm $C

Chinese blue & white

Dating from the late 17th century, this blue and white teapot is made from hard-paste porcelain, manufactured from rock or clay such as that found at the Jingdezhen kilns in northern China. When fired, the clay vitrifies into a fine white translucent ware, the porcelain so sought after by the Europeans.

The wares were decorated with traditional Chinese patterns and designs, reinterpreted to appeal to export markets. The painted underglaze cobalt blue decoration, which to modern eyes seems so typically Chinese, originated in Persia, as did the cobalt itself.

The fluted panels and bail handle derive from a metal original, which would probably have been decorated with a similar design in molded or hammered raised relief.

Height 8in/20cm $D

Chinese Imari

THE PALETTE OF COLORS WITH WHICH
this early 18th-century six-sided porcelain teapot
is decorated is very familiar to Europeans.
Known as Imari, it always consists of the
combination of blue, red, and gilt.

THE NAME IMARI ORIGINATED IN JAPAN, WHERE THIS
type of decoration was applied to wares from
the late 17th century onward. Quick to realize that
Japanese porcelain decorated in these colors found
a ready market with the Europeans, the Chinese
soon imitated it. Chinese genre scenes are painted on
both sides of this teapot, and there are bands of
hatched decoration at the foot and the neck.

ITS PORCELAIN COVER HAS BEEN LOST AT SOME POINT,
and a proud owner has had a silver
replacement made which is secured to the pot by
a chain – a typical arrangement in the 18th century.
The spout, too, is tipped with silver.

H c.6in/15cm $C

Chinese armorials

*A*LTHOUGH THIS GLOBULAR PORCELAIN TEAPOT,
*which dates from c.1750, is Chinese, it appears
quite European. Indeed, the round shape probably
derives from a European silver original, and
the teapot is decorated with a coat of arms. Such
wares, known as armorial porcelain, were
made expressly for the export market.*

*P*ORCELAIN WAS BEING MADE IN EUROPE BY THE 18TH
*century, and there were several factories operating
in Germany and France, such as Meissen and
Sèvres, but it was still more expensive and difficult
to obtain than the Chinese product. So
demand continued among the aristocracy of
Europe for Chinese porcelain.*

*T*HE NOBLE FAMILY TO WHICH THIS TEAPOT BELONGED
*would have sent a sketch of their coat of arms to
China – probably to Canton – where Chinese
decorators would have copied it carefully onto a tea
service or, possibly, an entire dinner service.*

Height 5½in/14cm $D

Yixing armorial

THIS YIXING POTTERY TEAPOT WAS MADE FOR *the European market and carries the coat of arms of a European family. It is uncommon for several reasons. Yixing teapots do not normally carry maker's marks, but impressed seals on the base of this one give both the maker's name, Shao Xuamao, and the former name of Yixing, Jingqi; it is also unusual to see a gilt armorial on a red-ware teapot. The shape is typically Chinese, rather than derived from a European or Middle Eastern source.*

THE TEAPOT CAN BE DATED TO THE LATE 17TH *or early 18th century, since it is known that Shao Xuamao was working at that time.*

Width 13in/33cm $E

Coats of arms in gilt are not commonly found on red ware, but they often occur on other types of porcelain.

Chinese famille rose

*MANUFACTURED FOR THE EUROPEAN MARKET
in the late 18th century, this porcelain teapot has
a classic globular shape, which may derive from that
of a contemporary European silver piece.
The handle is molded with a little scroll thumb
rest, which makes it easier to hold.*

*THE PORCELAIN IS PAINTED WITH BOUQUETS OF FLOWERS
in a type of decoration that uses what are
known as overglaze enamel colors. These were
made from metallic oxides and were painted on the
teapot after it had been glazed and fired once.
The name given to this particular palette
of colors,* famille rose, *refers to the pink that
occurs in the decoration, which came
into use only after c.1700.*

*AS COLORED OVERGLAZE ENAMELS REQUIRE THE
work of skilled painters as well as a time-consuming
and possibly damaging second firing,
colored wares have always been more expensive
and desirable to collectors.*

Height 5½in/14cm $B

Japanese blue & white

THE JAPANESE WERE UNABLE TO PRODUCE
*porcelain until about 1600, since a suitable clay
could not be found in Japan; so, much like
the Europeans, they depended on the Chinese
product. When they were eventually able to make
porcelain – mostly at kilns at Arita in
northern Kyushu – the ware was fine, hard, and
white, and of such good quality that it became
much sought by Europeans. However,
relations with Japan were difficult at times,
and on occasion the Japanese government would
close off all trade with Europe.*

SINCE THE JAPANESE HAD BEEN IMPORTING CHINESE
*porcelain for centuries, their designs often showed
a strong Chinese influence. Yet they also
produced designs such as this teapot purely with the
European market in mind. Although the scenes
on the teapot, made c.1700, look Oriental, they are
actually taken from Dutch engravings.*

Height 6in/15cm $F

Japanese Kakiemon

A FAMILY OF DECORATORS WORKING AT THE
*Arita kilns in the 17th century gave its name to the
porcelain known as Kakiemon. The term refers
to a type of overglaze decoration using a particular
palette of enamel colors, which are often
translucent. The palette is related to that of Imari,
but it is more subtle. It is based on red, green,
and blue coloration and often contains a
bright, distinctive yellow; some designs are lightly
outlined in black. Only when these colors
are present and the style of painting is correct
is the term properly used.*

*K*AKIEMON DECORATION – USUALLY SPRAYS OF FLOWERS,
*such as the chrysanthemum detail below, or birds in
flight – is most delicately painted. The wares were
much sought in Europe and, because of the
fine quality of the decoration, were
among the most expensive.
This teapot dates from c.1680.*

Height 4¾in/12cm $E

Japanese Imari

Imari decoration evolved at the Arita kilns in the early 1700s, at the same time as Kakiemon. The cobalt blue was put on under the glaze, and the red color (from iron oxide) over the glaze. Gilt, the final element, necessitated a third firing, which made these wares expensive. They were, nevertheless, very popular with Europeans.

Imari seen in Europe tends to date either from the early 18th century, as with the teapot shown here, or from the second half of the 19th century, since these were the periods when trade with Japan was at its height. Although the style of decoration maintained the same basic elements, the break of almost 150 years produced marked differences: the earlier wares are more delicately painted, while later pieces seem to have denser decoration. Gilding on the older wares is also of a richer, more burnished hue than that on the later ones.

Height 4in/10cm $C

Japanese Satsuma

USUALLY CALLED SATSUMA AFTER ITS PLACE OF origin, this type of pottery is a soft, cream-colored earthenware and was principally used for highly ornamental and decorative pieces. Shapes are frequently novel, and most of the decoration is overglaze and is generally delicately painted. The artists and potters often signed their wares.

THE RICH COLORS AND LARGE QUANTITIES OF GILDING, coupled with picturesque Japanese subjects of exotic flowers and birds, geishas, and so on, were not traditional native Japanese taste at all, but were designed purely for the European and American markets once trade with the West had opened up in the second half of the 19th century. Today Satsuma is collected by both Westerners and the Japanese, who are rediscovering an element of their past.

Height 7in/18cm $D

Delft

*UNTIL THE EARLY 1700S, THE CLOSEST EUROPEAN
potters came to porcelain was tin-glazed earthenware,
or faience. A vessel was commonly dipped into a
thick glaze containing tin oxide and then decorated
in cobalt blue. When the piece was fired, the fine
glossy white finish was like that of porcelain.*

*HUGE QUANTITIES OF THIS POTTERY WERE MADE AT DELFT
Holland, which gave its name to all such blue and
white wares, although they were made all over Europe;
the teapot above was made at Liverpool, mid-1700s.*

Height 6in/15cm $D

*IN THE EARLY 1600S, MUCH CHINESE PORCELAIN
was shipped into Holland,
where potters copied the
designs. The two Delft
teapots (1680–92) on the right
are rare shapes, taken directly
from Chinese examples.
Overglaze enamels
accentuate the underglaze
blue on the pot far right.*

Height 6¾in/17cm $E (both)

German faience

IN FRANCE, BRITAIN, AND GERMANY, THERE WERE
factories and entire towns specializing in the
production of tin-glazed earthenwares. The teapot
above was made c.1740 at Bayreuth, in Bavaria,
which from medieval times had had a tradition
of manufacturing pottery and stoneware.
From the early 18th century, it was one of the
main producers of faience in the area.

TIN-GLAZED EARTHENWARE WAS WELL SUITED FOR
decoration in colors and gilt as well as the simple
cobalt blue. When decorated in colors, a tin-glazed
piece would be fired, then painted over the glaze. It
is evident that the decorator who
painted the teapot above was
copying Chinese famille rose
porcelain, since he has attempted
to reproduce the colors
and delicate style of the
painting. The shape and
the strapwork on handle and
spout derive from silver examples.
Height 6in/15cm $F

Red stoneware

*T*HE ALCHEMIST *J*OHANN *F*RIEDRICH *B*ÖTTGER
was initially employed by Augustus the Strong, king
of Poland and elector of Saxony, in the hope
that he would be able to make gold.
Böttger set to work and, in about 1707, succeeded
instead in producing a fine red stoneware,
which he called jasper after the semiprecious stone.
Since this stoneware was fairly hard, it could be
cut and engraved, and marks still visible on the body
of this teapot, which dates from c.1715, indicate
that it was turned on a lathe.
   *T*HE RED CLAY BODY OF THE TEAPOT LOOKS MUCH
like the red Yixing teapots, but the rounded shape,
based on that of a silver example, and the
classical modeling of the mask at the spout, are
strongly European in style.
Height 5½in/14cm $G

Böttger porcelain

*I*N 1708 BÖTTGER STUMBLED ACROSS THE SECRET
*of making true hard-paste porcelain. His discovery
met with great acclaim, and in 1710 Augustus
founded a factory at Meissen, outside Dresden,
launching Böttger into production.*
*P*ORCELAIN WAS DIFFICULT AND EXPENSIVE TO MAKE, SO IT WAS
*regarded as a precious substance and, to start
with, designs were taken from European designs
for other such substances – namely gold and
silver – or from Chinese porcelain.*
*T*HIS TEAPOT, MADE C.1720, WAS BASED ON A CHINESE
blanc-de-Chine *original. Blanc-de-Chine is simple
unadorned white porcelain, deemed to be beautiful
in its own right without the need for further
decoration. Sometimes plain white porcelain was
gilded, although this has often worn off over time.*
Height 4½in/11.5cm $F

Vienna porcelain

MANY OF THE CRAFTSMEN AT MEISSEN MOVED
*elsewhere and spread the secret of making porcelain.
The teapots shown here were made c.1720–25
in Vienna at the Du Paquier factory, a competitor
to Meissen set up in 1718 under the patronage
of the Habsburg emperor Charles VI.*

THE VIENNA FACTORY WAS NOT JUST A PALE IMITATION OF
*Meissen; it contributed much to stylistic innovation and
evolution. The European-type decoration on the handle
of the teapot above, known as* Laub- und Bandelwerk
*(leaf and strapwork), was probably
copied from silver pots and was
a specialty of
the factory.
The decoration
on the lower
pot is an
interpretation of
Chinese art, with
the figures depicted
in a pictureseque manner.*

Heights 6in/15cm $F (top); $E (left)

Venetian chinoiserie

Between 1720 and 1727, hard-paste porcelain was produced at the Vezzi factory in Venice using kaolin (china clay) supplied directly from the Meissen clay pits in a cooperative venture with one of the chemists working at Meissen. When this support ended, Vezzi had to close. Northern Italy was under strong German and Austrian influence during this period, which explains such links.

The charm of this rare teapot, dating from 1725, lies in its so-called chinoiserie decoration, but other Vezzi wares are sometimes less well-decorated. European customers for such wares had a taste for the exotic, and the characters shown on the teapot are garbed in an amalgam of Turkish and other Oriental dress. There is also a hint of the costumes of the Italian Commedia dell'Arte, which was to make a significant impression on the work of artists and modelers farther north in Europe.

Height 6in/15cm $G

Meissen Kakiemon

IN THE LATE 1720s, AUGUSTUS THE STRONG,
elector of Saxony, began planning a fabulous
Japanese palace to be built at Dresden, and as a result
the influence of Japanese porcelain was profound
at the Meissen factory in the early days.
Meissen porcelain was hard and white, and copies
are very close to the Japanese original.
The decoration on this teapot, dating from c.1730,
imitates the Japanese Kakiemon palette; the shape
is also based on a Japanese example.

Height 4¼in/11cm $E

MEISSEN WARES ARE COMMONLY CLEARLY MARKED WITH
crossed swords. This (and the royal AR cipher) is the
most copied porcelain mark and appears on thousands
of pieces with no association with Meissen.

The crossed swords
used between
1730 and 1740 have
short blades and
broad hilts; the
number is that of
the gilder.

Meissen chinoiserie

*Böttger died in 1719, leaving one of the
greatest legacies in the production of porcelain,
although he never succeeded in establishing proper
decorators' workshops at Meissen, and the wares
were mostly decorated by outside workers. Much was
sent to Augsburg to be ornamented in gilt there.
In 1720, Johann Höroldt was recruited to the Meissen
factory as the chief decorator. He had acquired
his skills at the Du Paquier factory in Vienna,
and this teapot shows the typical* Laub- und
Bandelwerk *for which that factory was well known.
Höroldt favored chinoiserie scenes of figures
in exotic dress. Initially he copied from engravings,
but he soon evolved his own designs, and
his original, slightly overblown figures acquired a
character and individuality of their own.
This teapot was made c.1723.*
Height 5¼in/13.5cm $G

Meissen japonaiserie

Johann Joachim Kändler joined the Meissen factory in 1731. Trained as a sculptor, he was summoned by Augustus the Strong to work for him at the time when Augustus was obsessed with his Japanese palace. Although this existed only in the form of drawings and plans, Augustus was determined to see it become reality.

Kändler proved an inspired choice. He managed to overcome the technical difficulty of large pieces of porcelain "slumping" (altering shape) in the kiln when fired at the requisite high temperatures, as well as the artistic problem of producing the big, often life-size, models of birds and animals that the design required. His sculptures in porcelain, especially those of animals, are now regarded as among the most accomplished ever produced. That they were executed in a new and difficult medium makes them all the more astonishing.

These novelty teapots in the shape of a rooster and a hen were designed c.1731 and are probably meant to be Japanese jungle fowl.

Length 6in/15cm $G

Meissen deutsche Blumen

IN THE EARLY 18TH CENTURY, THERE WERE TWO main sources of design inspiration for teapots made in Europe. Many consciously copied Oriental examples; others, like this one, were based on European silver teapots. The decoration on this piece, however, although it is in tune with other mid-18th century decoration such as that found in wall paintings and embroidery, had never before been seen on ceramics.

ALONGSIDE HIS MORE EXOTIC DECORATIONS, JOHANN Höroldt at Meissen is credited with the development of this type of flower painting on porcelain, which became extremely popular. It is known as deutsche Blumen (German flowers), but the panels that actually enclose the flowers are still somewhat Oriental in shape.

THE PALE TURQUOISE GROUND ON WHICH THE DECORATION IS painted is a subtle color difficult to achieve in porcelain enamels. The teapot, made c.1750, demonstrates how far such painting had developed since porcelain was first made at Meissen.

Width 7in/18cm $C

Vincennes

WARES MADE AT THE FACTORY OF VINCENNES,
*to the west of Paris, became of such importance to
Louis XV that he decided that the factory
should be located closer to the court at Versailles,
and in 1756 it was moved to Sèvres.*
IN FACT, FROM 1745 THE ROYAL FLEUR-DE-LYS APPEARED
*on the porcelain, and in 1753 Vincennes began
to use the royal cipher and a date letter, establishing
a tradition of marking that is still used today
at Sèvres. Although the double "L" mark is one
of the most copied in the world, the collector
can usually identify a genuine piece by
comparing the painter's and other marks with the
factory mark and date code.*
THIS TEAPOT, MADE IN 1754, IS A MINIATURE
only a couple of inches high. **SC**

The interlaced "L's",
for Louis, became the mark
for both Vincennes and
Sèvres. Here the date letter
"B," for 1754, appears
within the mark.

Sèvres I

THE VINCENNES, LATER SÈVRES, FACTORY USED
soft-paste porcelain for its wares. The clay for
this does not occur naturally, but is usually a mixture
of white clay, ground glass, and flint that has been
calcined, or heated until it crumbles.

PORCELAIN OF THIS TYPE WAS MADE IN ITALY IN THE 1500s
and in France, at Rouen and St. Cloud, in the
late 1600s. The factory founded by
Prince Henri de Bourbon at Chantilly in 1726
used the St. Cloud porcelain recipe, and in
1738 the Vincennes factory arose, using the skills
developed at Chantilly. Installed at Sèvres
in 1756, this factory benefited from the interest of
the king and other wealthy patrons. The best
painters, modelers, and technicians
were engaged to produce truly artistic wares in
porcelain of the highest quality.

A DELIBERATE ATTEMPT WAS MADE TO BREAK FREE FROM
earlier traditions and to create new, lighter
fashions, as is evident in this cabaret set, delicately
painted with flowers and made in 1765.

Width tray 12¾in/32.5cm   Set $F; teapot $C

Sèvres II

A WELL-ESTABLISHED SYSTEM FOR THE TRAINING
and regulation of craftsmen existed at Sèvres.
A teapot such as this was thrown on the wheel by
one potter, the spout and handle made by
another, and the pieces assembled by a "repairer."
After the first firing, one decorator laid on the
ground color and another painted the
flowers. Following a second firing, the gilding was
applied and the teapot was fired again.

*D*ECORATORS' AND GILDERS' MARKS CAN OFTEN BE FOUND
on the base of a piece, and since records were kept of
the identities of the painters and their specialties,
a full picture has been built up of the factory's work.

*T*HIS TEAPOT, WITH ITS OVOID BODY, SHAPED SPOUT,
ear-shaped handle, and high round lid, is typical of
Sèvres. It can be dated to 1777 on the basis
of the marks and the colors used in the decoration.

Height 5½in/14cm $C

Frankenthal porcelain

*THIS TEAPOT WAS MADE AT FRANKENTHAL
in southern Germany in a factory which had been
established in 1754 by Paul Hannong.
It was bought by the Elector Palatinate, later
Prince Carl Theodor, who wished to produce his
own porcelain for courtly use and for
commercial exploitation.
MADE IN 1760 AS PART OF A CABARET SET – A TEA SET
with a tray – the pot was painted using
a pointillist technique, possibly by the artist Jacob
Osterspey, with a classical scene showing Venus and
Cupid. The mark on the base is a crowned "CT"
monogram (for Carl Theodor) in underglaze blue.
This mark quite often appears on copies,
sometimes in different colors from the original.
A much rarer mark used by the factory was
a lion rampant beneath a crown.*

Height 4in/10.5cm $E

English red ware

IN THE MID-17TH CENTURY, THERE WERE
*about 300 pottery factories in Staffordshire,
England, an area which had a long-standing history
of pottery production and a high reputation
for quality wares and good potters. This reputation
was further enhanced in the 18th century
during the Industrial Revolution.*

THE TYPE OF RED POTTERY BODY AND THE STYLE OF
*decoration of this teapot, which dates from 1775,
are quite clearly copied from Chinese Yixing
stoneware. A potter would have carved a "master"
model and parts of the pot would have been
made in molds taken from this model – the body
in two halves and the spout and handle
separately – and then have been assembled prior
to firing. The pot was, therefore, one of a
group of wares that was, literally, mass produced.
Despite this, few of these teapots have
survived, and this one is quite rare.*

Height 4¾in/12cm $D

Solid agate ware

THIS TEAPOT WAS MADE IN STAFFORDSHIRE
at about the same time as the red-ware example
opposite. Typically for Staffordshire, it is made from
pottery, and it is known that many potters
produced exactly the same model, so the maker
cannot be precisely identified.
THE UNUSUAL SHAPE, WHICH MAY HAVE BEEN COPIED
from a contemporary silver original, was intended
to represent a scallop shell. The raw material from
which the teapot was made was composed of
many different colored clays mixed together and
then pressed into a shell-shaped mold. This
type of pottery is known as solid agate ware, since it
was made in an attempt to imitate that
semiprecious stone. It is only one example of the
many different decorative techniques, often quite
innovative, developed by potters at the time.
Height 5½in/14cm $D

Tortoiseshell glaze

THE GLOBULAR, THREE-LEGGED BODY
and the bird finial on the cover of this teapot, made
in Staffordshire c.1750, are similar to those
found in silver teapots of the period.
The body of the pot was thrown – raised by hand
on a spinning potter's wheel – in the
traditional manner, while the spout and handle
were made in molds. The decoration of scrolling
flowers and vines was applied by hand,
although some elements, such as the flowers, would
have been made in small molds.
THOMAS WHIELDON, A PROLIFIC AND INNOVATIVE POTTER,
is sometimes credited with the development
of the type of streaked and colored
glazes that are simply poured on and constitute
the chief element of the decoration of this pot.
They are thought to resemble tortoiseshell
and give the ware its name.
Height 4½in/11.5cm $C

Saltglazed stoneware I

*PORCELAIN WAS RARE AND EXPENSIVE
in Europe in the middle of the 18th century.
Since Staffordshire potters did not initially
have the techniques and materials to manufacture
the genuine article, they made white
stoneware in imitation of porcelain. White clay
from southern England was mixed with
ground, heat-treated flints to form a material
that could be finely modeled.
Vessels were then fired at a temperature of
more than 1,800°F/1,000°C, and ordinary salt,
which oxidized to form the glaze,
was thrown into the kiln.*

*THIS UNUSUAL ENGLISH TEAPOT IN THE SHAPE OF A
recumbent camel, with a howdah on its back
molded with Chinese figures in panels, dates from
the mid-18th century. It was a novelty even in
its own time and is extremely rare today.*

Height 6in/15cm $F

Saltglazed stoneware II

*D*ATING FROM C.*1750*, THESE TWO
*Staffordshire teapots are among the many made at
this time from white saltglazed stoneware.*
*T*HE STONEWARE HERE HAS BEEN DECORATED IN IMITATION
of Chinese famille-rose *porcelain, using
overglaze enamel colors made from metallic oxides,
which are similar to those used on other types
of pottery and porcelain teapots.*
*S*INCE THIS TYPE OF DECORATION REQUIRED THE
*services of an additional craftsman and
also an extra firing, such pieces were
always more expensive.*
*The three-legged
shape is probably
based on a silver
original. Teapots of this
shape were available in a
wide variety of ceramic
bodies and many
different colored glazes.*
Height 4½in/11.5cm $E (both)

Chelsea I

A NOVELTY IN THE CHINESE TASTE, THIS PLAIN
white teapot is one of only four known to exist.
It was made between 1745 and 1749, at a factory in
Chelsea, London, from the artificial, or soft-paste,
porcelain then used at English factories.
IT IS PROBABLE THAT THE RECIPE FOR SUCH PORCELAIN,
which included ground glass, was brought to
England from France, since the factory was
founded and funded by a group of businessmen,
French émigrés among them. The English
upper classes were eager to buy porcelain, and
this new homemade product found a ready
market as a luxury commodity.
THE TEAPOT CARRIES THE INCISED TRIANGLE USED BY THE
Chelsea factory to mark its wares at the time.
Height 7in/17.5cm \$G

Chelsea II

THE DESIGN OF THIS LEAF-MOLDED CHELSEA
teapot, which was made beween 1745 and 1749,
is probably based on a shape originally
produced at Meissen. Emphasis on shapes derived
from nature was a feature of the Rococo style
that was popular in the 18th century.

MEISSEN PORCELAIN WAS KNOWN IN ENGLAND AT
the time, but it was prohibitively expensive to buy,
since heavy duties designed to discourage foreign
imports were levied on it. Nevertheless, such
porcelain was known to be the height of fashion in
the rest of Europe so, seeking to satisfy a
fashionable London clientele, the Chelsea factory
reproduced Meissen's designs.

THE DECORATION, WHICH ALSO IMITATES THAT
on Meissen pieces, would not have been
applied to the plain porcelain at the factory,
but in the workshop of an independent
decorator based in London.

Height 4¾in/12cm $G

Bow

*I*N ABOUT 1746, ROUGHLY THE SAME TIME
*as the factory at Chelsea was established, a rival
concern was set up in Bow in east London.*
*W*HEREAS CHELSEA WAS PATRONIZED BY AN ARISTOCRATIC
*clientele, notably the Duke of Cumberland, Bow
aimed its wares at a more middle-class,
less sophisticated market. The porcelain was
frequently advertised as being durable, not
susceptible to cracking at high temperatures, and
thus eminently suitable for teawares. This
was because Bow's recipe for soft-paste porcelain
contained bone ash, a phosphate which
produces a strong porcelain body.*
*T*HE MAIN DESIGN INSPIRATION AT THE BOW FACTORY WAS
*Oriental – indeed the factory was initially
called New Canton. The designs, such as the one
shown here, imitated many Chinese and
Japanese examples, and the factory was known
especially for its blue and white porcelain.*
Height 3¼in/8.5cm $C

Pineapple shape

*THIS POTTERY TEAPOT IS A GOOD EXAMPLE
of the 18th-century obsession with
novelty. The wealthy tea-drinking classes liked to
decorate their tables with exotic forms,
whether they were designs in the Chinese taste
or unusual naturalistic ones.*

*IN 1760, WHEN THIS TEAPOT WAS MADE, A PINEAPPLE
was an exotic, rare, and expensive fruit. Since
it was also the symbol of hospitality
(18th-century houses often had pineapple finials
on the gateposts), it was particularly suited
to a design for a teapot – tea being the perfect way
to welcome honored guests.*

*IT IS POSSIBLE THAT THE TEAPOT WAS MADE BY
Josiah Wedgwood. Although not marked, the
pottery is of the high quality expected from him,
and similar marked examples are known.*

Height 5¼in/13.5cm $E

Wedgwood creamware

ALTHOUGH THESE TEAPOTS ARE NOT MARKED, *they can be identified by the shape of the finials on the covers and that of the handles and spouts as having been produced c.1770 in Josiah Wedgwood's factory in Staffordshire. They are made of creamware, a fine white pottery similar in composition to stoneware but fired at a lower temperature.*

WEDGWOOD TRAINED IN THE STAFFORDSHIRE *potteries, notably under Thomas Whieldon, one of the most gifted mid-18th century potters. In 1759 Wedgwood established his own pottery, making wares primarily for domestic use. He quickly realized that the fashionable London market was the most lucrative and set up a decorating workshop there run by David Rhodes, who painted these teapots before they went for sale.*

Height both 5in/13cm $D

William Greatbatch

*ANOTHER NOTABLE STAFFORDSHIRE POTTER
was William Greatbatch. His work has only recently
been recognized, as a result of the excavation
of the site of his pottery. Previously he was thought
to have been an engraver or designer, since
his name appears in the transfer prints on items
such as this creamware teapot, which shows
a fortune teller on one side of the pot and
a zodiacal chart on the other.
NOW THAT MORE IS KNOWN ABOUT GREATBATCH'S WORK,
it has been discovered that he worked for
Wedgwood on occasion, helping make up quantities
of creamware teapots for large orders when
Wedgwood did not have enough in stock.
Greatbatch's designs were his own, however, as
this distinctively shaped pot with its
ear-shaped handle demonstrates. The print on
the teapot carries the date 1778.*

Height 5in/13cm $E

Transfer-printed creamware

Long may we Live,
Happy may we be,
Blest with Content,
And from Misfortunes free.

THIS UNMARKED CREAMWARE TEAPOT, MADE
c.1770, *can be accurately attributed to Josiah
Wedgwood on the basis of its shape. Although
Wedgwood did not invent creamware, he popularized
it, and as a result of his commission for a
creamware tea service for Queen Charlotte, it became
the most fashionable of wares. Previously only
porcelain or silver had been regarded as suitable
for use by royalty or the aristocracy.*

DURING THE EARLY 18TH CENTURY, ATTEMPTS HAD
*been made to perfect a technique of transfer
printing on pottery and porcelain. Then,
in 1756, John Sadler and Guy Green patented
a process in which paper printed with the design in
metallic oxides was wrapped around the piece
and burnt away in the kiln, leaving the pattern on
the glaze. They set up a business in Liverpool,
where this teapot was decorated.*

Height 4¾in/12cm $C

Liverpool porcelain

Dᴜʀɪɴɢ ᴛʜᴇ 18ᴛʜ ᴄᴇɴᴛᴜʀʏ, Lɪᴠᴇʀᴘᴏᴏʟ was an important shipping and trading city. It was also a significant center for the production of ceramics, initially blue and white English delft, and, from the mid-18th century, porcelain.

Pᴏʀᴄᴇʟᴀɪɴ ᴏꜰ ᴀ ᴛʏᴘᴇ ʀᴏᴜɢʜʟʏ sɪᴍɪʟᴀʀ ᴛᴏ ᴛʜᴀᴛ ᴍᴀᴅᴇ by Worcester and other English companies was produced in a number of factories in Liverpool, notably those of Richard Chaffer and Philip Christian, who was Chaffer's partner and took over his shapes, patterns, and porcelain formula. The porcelain was soft paste and was seldom pure white, but had a pleasant blue, greenish, or gray cast.

Tʜɪs ᴛᴇᴀᴘᴏᴛ ᴡᴀs ᴍᴀᴅᴇ ᴀᴛ Cʜʀɪsᴛɪᴀɴ's ꜰᴀᴄᴛᴏʀʏ ᴄ.1760. The shape is similar to a design produced at Worcester, while the molding is of good quality, the potting thin and crisp, and the painted chinoiserie decoration, with its yellow, green, and characteristic mauve-purple, is bright and colorful.

Height 5in/13cm $D

Worcester porcelain

IN 1751 A FACTORY WAS ESTABLISHED AT WORCESTER
*to produce porcelain and it became one of the best
factories in Britain. Although the porcelain contained
soap rock mined from Cornish kaolin deposits, it was
still soft paste, as was most English porcelain.
But its consistently high quality made it particularly
suitable for holding hot liquids and it was,
therefore, ideal for tea and coffee wares.*
MUCH OF THE OUTPUT WAS PAINTED AT THE FACTORY IN
*underglaze blue, with designs that copied Chinese
originals, but many porcelain blanks, such as the
teapot above, were sent to London for decoration.*
Height *c.*5in/12.5cm $C

THE TEAPOT ON THE
*right, made c.1760,
was perhaps meant
to match other
Oriental porcelain
already owned by the
family whose arms its bears.*
Height 4¾in/12cm $E

Wedgwood & Bentley

Between 1769 and 1780, Josiah Wedgwood worked in close collaboration with a businessman and friend named Thomas Bentley. Bentley was a man of taste, and being based in London, was ideally placed to inform Wedgwood of the latest fashions. The partnership produced principally ornamental wares, and this teapot carrying the partnership's impressed mark is a rarity.

The stoneware body contains iron oxide which gives it the black color. This type of ceramic body, called black basalt or basaltes, was developed by Wedgwood, who was extremely proud of his creation. It was a hard, unglazed body capable of taking fine molding and applied relief decoration. The teapot is painted in matte overglaze enamels in imitation of ancient Greek pottery, a technique known as encaustic decoration.

Height 5in/13cm $E

Turner caneware

THE POTTER JOHN TURNER SET UP HIS FACTORY
at Lane End in Staffordshire in the early 1760s.
Working with his sons, he soon established a
reputation for fine-quality earthenware. The wares
produced by the Turners are of a quality comparable
to that of Wedgwood, and the pieces were always
well potted – that is, carefully and precisely made.
DATING FROM C.1790, THIS TEAPOT IS IN AN UNGLAZED
buff-colored pottery known as caneware, since
it was thought to have the color and texture
of bamboo. It is of a refined and delicate
classically inspired design, with decoration in
blue enamel accentuating the pale pottery.
TURNER HAD LONDON SHOWROOMS, AS DID WEDGWOOD,
in which a teapot such as this, intended for the
wealthy, would have been displayed.
Height 6in/15cm $D

Spode caneware

*J*OSIAH SPODE, ANOTHER NOTABLE
*Staffordshire potter, established his factory
c.1770. Unlike manufacturers such as Wedgwood
and Turner, Spode did not confine his production
to pottery but, in the 1790s, produced a type of
porcelain that contained bone ash – the
famous bone china. This was immensely popular
for tea services, since it withstood heat
exceptionally well and seldom cracked.*
*O*THER QUALITY CERAMIC BODIES INCLUDED IRONSTONE, OR
*"stone china," and Spode's hand-engraved blue
and white transfer-prints on pottery and porcelain
are among the most collectable wares today.*
*T*HIS SQUARE-SECTION CHINESE-STYLE TEAPOT, DATING FROM
*c.1790, was made in caneware and is enriched
with blue and white enamels. It is marked "Spode"
in impressed letters on the base.*
Height 6in/15cm $C

Wedgwood jasperware

IN 1776 WEDGWOOD PERFECTED A PROCESS
*by which the stoneware body could be tinted in
delicate colors by the addition of metallic oxides.
Blue, achieved by staining the body with
cobalt blue, was most common, but he also
produced shades of green and yellow. Wedgwood
called this new product jasperware after the
semiprecious stone. Since the coloring ingredients
were expensive, they were made to go a long way,
and after c.1780 pieces with a solid white body
were simply dipped in a colored slip.*

THIS TEAPOT, MADE IN 1785, IS A PERFECT EXAMPLE
*of the high level of workmanship achieved
by Staffordshire potters in the late 18th century.
It is of stoneware, which was well suited
to being delicately worked. The contrasting frieze
of figures and the spout and handle were
applied later. The flutes at the base were incised
through to the base color.*

Height 4¼in/11cm $D

English Imari I

ONE OF THE BEST-KNOWN TYPES OF DECORATION
on English porcelain is the Imari pattern,
based on the designs on Japanese porcelain, which
were thought to have been derived from
patterns for woven brocades. The Japanese used
these designs for ceramics intended to
appeal to European tastes, and during the
19th century the Imari palette of underglaze blue,
overglaze iron-red, and gilt elements was widely
copied in English factories.

THE SEVERE, STRAIGHT-SIDED OVAL NEWHALL TEAPOT
with its stand (above) dates from
c.1800; the shape is
typical of the period.

Height 6in/15cm $B

POSSIBLY MADE BY
Davenport, the small
single-person teapot
(left) dates from c.1810
and is of so-called Empire
shape. It incorporates green
into the Imari design.

Height 5in/13cm $B

English Imari II

IMARI PATTERNS ARE USUALLY COMPOSED OF traditional Oriental motifs of scrolling leaves and flowers such as peonies and chrysanthemums, but they are sometimes completely abstract. English factories developed their own patterns, varying the palette and the design, which might be hand painted or printed, or a combination of both.

THE DERBY "LONDON SHAPE" TEAPOT (ABOVE) DATES from c.1820. It is painted with a landscape on a blue and gilt ground that derives from Imari decoration.

Height 5½in/14cm $B

DATING FROM THE SECOND HALF OF THE 19TH CENTURY, the unusually shaped Derby teapot and stand (below) are decorated with the Imari-type pattern that today is commonly associated with this factory.

Height 5½in/14cm $B

Yellow pottery

As the Industrial Revolution spread throughout Britain during the 18th century, more and more potteries were set up to produce wares for a growing and increasingly prosperous population. And as tea became more affordable and the custom of tea drinking spread from the aristocracy to all classes of people, more humble teapots such as this were made to meet the demand.

The style of this teapot, with its straight spout, indicates that it was probably produced c.1810 in the north of England, possibly in Sunderland or Yorkshire. Although of a fairly mass-produced nature, it was, nevertheless, decorated by hand, the flowers and leaves being painted on with broad brush strokes. Since not many wares with this attractive bright yellow ground have survived, teapots of this type have become quite sought after.

Height 5½in/14cm $B

Newhall bone china

ALTHOUGH SPODE IS CREDITED WITH THE INVENTION *of bone china, it was the factory at Newhall in Staffordshire that brought bone-china tearwares to the masses. Originally a manufacturer of a type of artificial hard-paste porcelain, it began to make bone china some time after 1812. Newhall porcelain is satisfying to collect for anyone interested in patterns, since the factory produced a wide variety of attractive designs, and many pieces are clearly marked with an "N" followed by the pattern number.*

THIS "LONDON SHAPE" TEAPOT, WITH WICKER-MOLDED *borders, dates from 1820. It would originally have been part of a tea service and would have been fairly expensive, since it is painted and gilded, but less costly china tearwares were also produced.*

Height 5½in/14cm $B

Sèvres hard paste

FOR MOST OF THE 18TH CENTURY, THE PORCELAIN
made in France was of the soft-paste type.
The glossy, white hard paste made in Germany was,
however, widely admired, and the search for
deposits of kaolin (china clay) continued.

IN 1768 A DEPOSIT WAS FOUND AT LIMOUSIN; A YEAR LATER,
the Sèvres factory produced its first hard-paste wares
and was granted the exclusive right to produce the
porcelain. During the French Revolution (1789–94),
the factory got into financial difficulties and it
was taken into state ownership in 1793.

SINCE MUCH OF THE EARLY PORCELAIN WAS MADE FOR ROYAL
use, it was known as Royal Porcelain and a crown
was added to the usual marks. Soft-paste porcelain,
called French porcelain, continued to be made
and marked with the double "L" as before.

THIS TEAPOT IS IN THE NEOCLASSICAL STYLE, WHICH REPLACED
the Rococo in the mid-18th century. It carries
the date letters "NN" for 1791.

Height 6in/15cm $B

Paris porcelain

*T*HE TERM *P*ARIS PORCELAIN IS USED TO
*describe porcelain wares made in and around Paris
in the late 18th and early 19th centuries by
the many small factories that sprang up to supply
the post-Revolutionary bourgeoisie. There
were many of these concerns, often under the
patronage of aristocratic sponsors, eager to exploit
the waning influence of the Sèvres factory.
The porcelain was almost exclusively hard paste,
made from native kaolin deposits.*
*T*HESE FACTORIES OFTEN MARKED THEIR WARES WITH SINGLE
*incised letters or symbols, which makes
identification of the maker difficult. The shape and
design of pieces was, in general, rather uninspired or
based on Sèvres originals. Nevertheless, some, such
as this boldly decorated teapot dating from c.1820,
do have charm. The rather imprecise painting
suggests that it may have been sold as a blank by
the factory to a decorator's workshop.*
Height 6in/15cm $B

Twentieth-century Meissen

*THE DESIGN OF THIS MEISSEN TEAPOT,
which dates from the early 20th century, draws
heavily on its 18th- and 19th-century heritage, not
only in the shape of the body, but also in the
bark-molded spout and handle, the flower finial on
the cover, and the hand-painted decoration of
scattered flowers. The teapot is smaller than usual,
since it is meant for a single person.*

Height 4in/10.5cm **$B**

*MEISSEN CONTINUES TO MAKE WELL-CRAFTED GOOD-QUALITY
wares that reflect its long tradition as the leading
porcelain factory in Europe. A good guide to dating
is to examine the mark on the base of a piece – after
1900 the crossed swords and other marks are
carefully drawn and tend to be quite small.*

The Meissen
crossed swords
mark here dates
from 1910. It is
still in underglaze
blue, with a gilt
numeral.

Dresden porcelain

*MANY OTHER FACTORIES, SEEKING TO EMULATE
Meissen's wares, have grown up in its shadow,
and confusion exists in the minds of many people
between Meissen and Dresden.*

*THE CLOSEST LARGE CITY TO THE FACTORY AT
Meissen is Dresden. In consequence, Meissen
porcelain is seen as coming from Dresden, and
until relatively recently its wares were
often called Dresden porcelain. However, porcelain
made in that city has not necessarily been
made at the Meissen factory.*

*THIS TEAPOT DATES FROM THE EARLY YEARS
of the 20th century. Although it takes some of its
design inspiration from Meissen wares
and is of good quality, it is clearly marked on the
base with "Dresden" and a crown. This is a
decorator's mark, probably that of either Adolph
Hamann or Richard Klemm, who worked in
Dresden from the late 19th century until
the early 20th century. The hand-painted flowers
make this teapot a very attractive piece.*

Height 4¼in/11cm $B

Vienna porcelain

IN 1747, THE FACTORY FOUNDED BY DU PAQUIER
*in Vienna almost 30 years earlier, came under
the patronage of Empress Maria Theresa.
Popularly known as the Royal Vienna factory, it was
renowned for its lavish decoration, often of
classical scenes within colored geometric panels
enhanced with rich raised gilding.*

THE FACTORY WAS TAKEN OUT OF STATE OWNERSHIP IN 1864,
*since it was proving an expensive enterprise, and the
many decorators who had worked there were
forced to set up on their own. Technically, therefore,
after this date Vienna or Vienna-style porcelain was
the work of decorators working on blanks,
although it often carried the official factory mark
of a blue shield or a beehive. Frequently the
porcelain was still of exceptional quality, as this
signed teapot, dating from c.1900, demonstrates.*

Height 8¼in/21cm $D

Naples-style porcelain

DURING THE 18TH CENTURY, IT BECAME A matter of prestige for European royalty to have their own porcelain factories, and in 1771 one was set up at Naples for King Ferdinand. It became renowned for its classically styled wares, inspired by the excavations at Pompeii and Herculaneum, and it made many excellent copies of the decoration on objects that were found there. The royal factory closed down in 1806, but was revived for a short while under private ownership in 1807–34.

THE FACTORY MARK, A BLUE "N" UNDER A CROWN, IS one of those most frequently copied, and this teapot, which was probably made in Germany in the 19th century, carries such a mark. It is difficult to say with any certainty who made it, but the teapot, with its high-relief molded friezes of classical figures, clearly sets out to imitate the wares of the Naples factory. Because such pieces are extremely decorative, they have now become collectible in their own right.

Height 6in/15cm $B

Royal Worcester

IN THE LATER PART OF THE 19TH CENTURY,
there was a general dissatisfaction with
design ethics in Britain, and attempts were made at
reform, which led to the development of the
Arts and Crafts Movement.

CERTAIN INFLUENTIAL ARTISTS AND DESIGNERS, SUCH AS
James McNeill Whistler, looked farther afield for
their inspiration – to China and Japan. Known as the
Aesthetic Movement, this group was particularly
active in the 1870s and '80s, and the members
were especially interested in Oriental blue and white
porcelain, such as the large 17th-century
Chinese teapot above right. As interest spread and
demand grew, blue and white porcelain
was again imported in quantity.

Height 10¼in/26cm   \$D

FACTORIES SUCH AS ROYAL WORCESTER WERE QUICK
to catch onto this fashion, and many of their wares
began to be made in direct imitation of the
Oriental. The Royal Worcester teapot above left
was made between 1870 and 1880.

Height *c.*8in/20cm   \$B

Rozenburg

The influence of *Oriental* forms on *Western*
art in the late 19th century was immense, for it
liberated European artists from previously accepted
notions of design. Indeed, the Japanese interest
in nature encouraged the development of a style
directly based on natural forms. Known as
Art Nouveau, its lines often imitated the sinuous
curves seen in plant and animal life.
Strongly favored in *Continental* *Europe*, especially
in France and Belgium, Art Nouveau was also popular
in Britain and the United States. Each country
brought a unique flavor to the style, as is shown by
this distinctively shaped and decorated teapot, made
at the Rozenburg factory in the Netherlands c.1903.

Height *c.*10in/25cm   \$G

Printed mark *c.*1900
The teapot can be
dated by the
attribution of
the decoration to a
particular artist.

Belleek

WHEN CHINA CLAY WAS DISCOVERED AT BELLEEK,
*Ireland, it provided an opportunity to found a
factory in 1857 where none had previously existed.
The factory at first made pottery, but the local
clay was of such good quality that it was well suited
to the production of porcelain, and it is
for this, and notably parian (fine unglazed biscuit
porcelain), that Belleek is best known.*

THE SHAPES ARE NEARLY ALWAYS ORIGINAL, OFTEN BASED ON
*seashells and marine forms. This teapot, made c.1900,
shows an Oriental influence in its basket-weave
body, angular "bamboo" handle, griffin's-head
spout, and griffin's feet. The fine, creamy colored
porcelain is simply enriched with gilt.*

Height 6in/15cm $C

This printed mark
on the interior of the
cover of the teapot
provides instructions
on how to brew a pot
of tea without
damaging the pot.

Minton majolica

MAJOLICA IS THE ENGLISH FORM OF THE ITALIAN
word maiolica, *a term which refers to
traditional tin-glazed earthenwares made in Italy
from the 15th century onward. The name is
said to come from ceramics introduced to Italy
from the Spanish island of Majorca.*

VIVIDLY DECORATED ENGLISH MAJOLICA WAS MOLDED OR
*pressed to give sharp relief, but the bright
glazes were lead, not tin, based. It was made in
large quantities at potteries in Staffordshire,
production reaching its height in the
second half of the 19th century.*

THESE WARES WERE TECHNICALLY SUPERB AND FOUND A READY
*market. They exploited all the fashionable design
styles of the period, which were anything
from Neoclassical to Art Nouveau and Oriental in
inspiration – like this teapot. A typically witty,
light-hearted design, it was made c.1880 by Minton,
one of the greatest producers of majolica.*

Height 5in/13cm $D

Wemyss Ware

WEMYSS **W**ARE *IS ESSENTIALLY A BRAND NAME FOR a wide variety of pieces made by the factory of Robert Heron and Sons at Fife in Scotland. Most of the pieces were originally quite unexceptional, with domestic wares, especially bedroom sets, the main items of production.*

THE FACTORY WAS IN COMPETITION WITH A NUMBER OF *others in the area, and in order to capture a special niche in the market, Heron introduced a decorator from Bohemia by the name of Karl Nekola, who trained many local men. The principal form of decoration was flowers or fruit, but animals such as cocks, hens and pheasants also featured.*

WEMYSS **W**ARE SOLD EXTREMELY WELL, ESPECIALLY IN *London, where its "folksy" look became fashionable with the upper classes. This teapot, dating from c.1900, is painted in a fairly unusual manner, with bold brush strokes. Pieces decorated with fruit such as oranges or lemons, or flowers such as heather or harebells, are most collectable.*

Height *c.*4in/10cm $B

Barge style

*THIS TEAPOT IS OF A TYPE KNOWN AS BARGE STYLE
because of its rather naive flowery decoration,
which has been incorrectly linked with the type of
decoration that barge dwellers in England painted
on their boats and enamel pots. It is, in
fact, simply a kind of pottery widely made by
British factories in the 19th century.*

*SUCH TEAPOTS WERE NEARLY ALWAYS DATED AND INSCRIBED,
and their charm usually lies in the inscription.
They were almost always too large to be of practical
use, which suggests that they were made as gifts
and were intended for display only, and often carry
specially commissioned inscriptions or the names of
public houses, places, or particular individuals.
Large numbers of these teapots seem to have been
made between the 1860s and 1900, with the
result that they are still quite common.*

Height 10¼in/26cm $A

Foley "politician"

THIS TEAPOT IS MADE IN THE FORM OF A caricature of a late 19th-century politician named Sir William Harcourt; a colleague of William Gladstone, he was famous in his time as a reforming Liberal. It is one of a series of teapots representing famous politicians that were made by the Foley factory in Staffordshire c.1900. The shape of the teapots does not vary much, and the characterization of the different figures is provided by the underglaze outline design and colors.

PIONEERED BY FREDERICK RHEAD, ONE OF THE MOST famous and innovative designers associated with the Foley factory, this type of decoration was known as "intarsio." The technique proved to be hugely successful, principally on more decorative wares rather than on these humorous ones.

IN 1925 FOLEY WAS RENAMED SHELLEY POTTERIES, AND it produced rather beautiful and collectable tea sets in the Art Deco style during the 1920s and '30s.

Height 5in/13cm $B

Wartime wares

MADE IN STAFFORDSHIRE BY CROWN DUCAL
*to celebrate the Allied effort during World War II,
this teapot was probably designed before the war, in
the 1930s, when the shape would have served
as a vehicle for various promotional ventures, mostly
non-political advertising for tea companies.
During the war, little time, money, or resources were
available to produce innovative designs, and old ones
were revamped to suit new purposes.*

TEAPOTS, AS WELL AS MANY OTHER DOMESTIC WARES,
*have been printed with political slogans
since the 18th century, and such pieces can form the
basis of an interesting collection. The secret is
to seek out those that are rare or unusual.
Most 18th-century examples are extremely rare
in comparison to 20th-century items
such as this teapot; nevertheless, it is highly
collectible as a curiosity of its time.*

Height 5in/13cm \$B

Donald Duck

WADEHEATH IN STAFFORDSHIRE MADE THIS
*teapot in 1936 – it can be dated precisely from the
printed mark on the base. Donald Duck is
shown in one of his earliest incarnations, as he
emerged from the design studios of Walt Disney in
the 1930s. He was to change shape altogether
after World War II, being transformed from the very
ducklike creature of the 1930s, with a low body
and long neck – a shape perfectly suited to that
of a teapot – to today's upright, more human
character. A design such as this is generally thought
of as typical of the 20th century, but strongly
characterized bird forms had been used for teapot
designs in previous centuries.*

ALTHOUGH FACTORY MADE, THE TEAPOT WAS HAND
*painted and must have been quite an expensive
novelty in its time; it retains a great deal
of charm as a special period piece. Smaller versions
of this fairly large teapot also exist.*

Height *c*.6½in/17cm $B

Sabu & the elephant

COLCLOUGH CHINA, ANOTHER STAFFORDSHIRE *manufacturer, produced this teapot, which can be dated to the 1940s. This is partly because of the style of the printed mark on the base, which was used for only a few years, and partly because it represents a real individual, the Indian actor Sabu, who starred in movies of the period. Sabu was extremely popular, particularly in his role in Alexander Korda's version of Rudyard Kipling's* Toomai of the Elephants.

ALTHOUGH THIS PARTICULAR TEAPOT COULD ONLY HAVE BEEN *made in the 20th century, it is interesting to note that teapots made to exotic designs, such as the camel teapot shown on page 39, were produced in Staffordshire in the 18th century, which already showed a fascination with the Orient. Even the techniques of production, such as molding and slip-casting, have not changed substantially in the past 200 years.*

Height 5½in/14cm $A

Clarice Cliff

*THE NOTED DESIGNER CLARICE CLIFF WAS
born in Staffordshire in 1899. Like many young
people there, she went into the pottery industry
almost as a matter of course. Her first major
job was as an apprentice decorator at
A.J. Wilkinson's, whose manager, Colley Shorter,
saw her great potential and encouraged her.
By the 1920s, she had her own studio within
the factory, designing specialty lines.*

*CLIFF PRODUCED A HUGE QUANTITY OF TYPICAL ART DECO
patterns, which has made her wares highly collectible,
since they can be accumulated by
pattern. The "Conical"
shape teapot
(above) is painted in
the "Tennis" pattern,
and the "Stamford"
shape teapot (right) is
decorated in the
"Honolulu" pattern.*

Height above
*c.*5½in/14cm \$C;
right 5in/13cm \$C

Susie Cooper

ANOTHER WELL-KNOWN WOMAN POTTER,
*contemporary with Cliff, was Susie Cooper, who was
born at Burslem, Staffordshire, in 1902. She started
work at A.E. Gray & Co. Ltd. as a decorator;
then, in 1930, set up her own factory and was able
to design and produce whatever wares she chose.*
COOPER WAS ALWAYS CONCERNED WITH QUESTIONS OF
*utility, and her teapots were designed to pour well.
Initially, her decoration was strongly influenced
by the geometric designs of the 1930s, as this
teapot shows, and some of her early work is in
the strident colors typical of the period.
Later her palette became more muted and
subtle and the designs refined and delicate, while
retaining a strong individual character.*
HER FACTORY WAS BOUGHT BY WEDGWOOD IN 1966,
*and she worked for the company until retiring, when
she continued to work on her own.*
Height *c*.6¾in/17.5cm $B

Laura Knight

ALTHOUGH PRODUCED COMMERCIALLY, THIS TEAPOT
*was made from a design by the artist Dame Laura
Knight for an exhibition in 1934 at Harrods, the
London department store. The aim of the exhibition
was to raise the standard of British design in ceramic
and glass tablewares by bringing artists together
with the factories that produced these wares.*
A COLLABORATION WAS ESTABLISHED BETWEEN LAURA KNIGHT,
*who was principally a painter of circus and ballet
themes, and the designer Clarice Cliff at
A.J. Wilkinson's. The joint effort was fruitful;
for although Knight had little knowledge of the mass
production of ceramics, this design is not
simply surface decoration, but encompasses the
teapot's shape while retaining much of the character
of her work. The teapot did not, however, go into
mass production, which makes it rather rare.*

Height 7½in/19cm $E

Shaun Clarkson

*Intended primarily as a work of art, this
teapot was made by the artist Shaun Clarkson for an
exhibition at the Waldorf Hotel, London, in 1991.
The exhibition was staged jointly with Twinings,
a company that has traded in tea since 1706.
It included 50 teapots, celebrating various themes,
among them the international taste for tea
exemplified by the American design above.
Shaun Clarkson's work so far has concentrated on
household objects usually regarded as being
of little significance, and he has sought to reveal the
importance of such objects by elevating them
to the status of works of art. While this pot is new
both in design and concept, it confirms
an enduring passion for tea drinking, and for
the vessel that tea is brewed in.*

Height 6½in/17cm $C

Glossary

APPLIED DECORATION Ornament prepared in advance and added to a completed piece, as with Wedgwood's jasperware.

ARITA The name of the kilns at Kyushu, where most fine white hard-paste Japanese porcelain was produced from *c.*1600.

ARMORIAL PORCELAIN Name generally given to Chinese export wares painted with the coats of arms of European families.

BLANC-DE-CHINE French term for unpainted highly translucent Chinese porcelain characterized by a thick glaze.

BODY The mixture of raw materials from which pottery and porcelain are made.

CHINOISERIE Mid-18th century European style of decoration inspired by Chinese and Oriental decoration and design. Not to be confused with genuine Chinese articles exported to Europe.

FAIENCE Earthenware (pottery that is waterproof only when glazed) with a glaze whitened with oxide of tin. Also known as Delft (in Holland), delft (in England), and tin-glazed earthenware.

FAMILLE ROSE "Pink family"; overglaze enamel colors used on Chinese porcelain from *c.*1700, the predominant color being rose pink.

FAMILLE VERTE "Green family"; transparent enamels, particularly brilliant green, used to decorate Chinese porcelain. The best examples date from the late 17th and early 18th centuries.

HARD-PASTE PORCELAIN Porcelain made from kaolin (china clay) which, when fired, produces a fine white body.

IMARI A port in Japan which gave its name to the distinctive red, blue, and gilt decoration seen on Japanese porcelain and widely copied in the West from *c.*1700.

JAPONAISERIE European designs and style influenced by Japanese forms.

KAKIEMON Style of Japanese decoration, usually using red, green, blue, yellow, and sometimes black or deep purple, that took its name from a family of decorators at Arita. It became popular and was widely imitated in Europe.

OVERGLAZE ENAMELS Colored pigments made from metallic oxides painted or printed on ceramics after glazing. A second firing is required to fix them.

SOFT-PASTE PORCELAIN "Artificial" porcelain, usually containing refined white clays and sometimes ground glass.

STONEWARE A pottery body fired at a high temperature, which makes it impervious to liquids. It is hard, durable, and quite dense. By using different clays and including various metallic oxides, a wide range of colors can be produced, for example, Yixing red ware and Wedgwood black basalt.

Index

A

Aesthetic movement 64
agate ware 37
Arita 18, 19, 20
armorials 15, 16, 49
Art Deco 70, 74, 75
Art Nouveau 65, 67
Arts and Crafts
    Movement 64
Augsburg 29
Augustus the Strong,
    king of Poland and
    elector of Saxony 24,
    25, 28, 30

B

bail handle 7, 13
basalt, black 50
Belleek 66
Bentley, Thomas 50
blanc-de-Chine 25
bone china 52, 57
Böttger, Johann Friedrich
    24, 25, 29
Bow 43

C

cabaret sets 33, 35
caneware 51, 52
Canton 6, 15
Carl Theodor, Prince 35
Chaffer, Richard 48
Chantilly 33
Charles VI, Emperor 26
Chelsea factory 41, 42,
    43
china clay *see* kaolin
Chinese influence 9, 18,
    43, 44, 49, 52, 64
Chinese taste 21, 41, 44,
    64
chinoiserie 26, 27, 29,
    39, 48
Christian, Philip 48
Clarkson, Shaun 77

classical style 63
Cliff, Clarice 74, 76
cobalt blue 13, 20, 22,
    23
Colclough China 73
Cooper, Susie 75
creamware 45, 46, 47
Crown Ducal 71

D

Davenport factory 54
decoration
    applied 53
    blue and white 11, 13,
        18, 22, 43, 48, 52, 64
    encaustic 50
    floral 19, 31, 55
    hatched 14
    intarsio 70
    overglaze 17, 21, 22
    underglaze 12, 13, 22,
        35, 49
decorators' and gilders'
    marks 34
Delft 22
delft 9, 48
Derby 55
deutsche Blumen 31
Dresden 25, 28
Du Paquier factory 26,
    29, 62

E

earthenware
    lead-glazed 67
    tin-glazed 9, 22, 23,
        67

F

factory marks 28, 32, 35,
    41, 58, 59, 62, 63, 65,
    66, 73
faience 9, 22, 23
famille rose 17, 23, 40
finials 38, 44, 45

Foley factory 70
Frankenthal 35
French porcelain 58

G, H

geometric designs 75
gilding 20, 21, 23, 25,
    29, 34, 57, 62, 66
glazes
    salt 39, 40
    tortoiseshell 38
Gray, A.E. & Co. 75
Greatbatch, William 46
Hannong, Paul 35
Horemans, J.J. 7
Höroldt, Johann 29, 31

I, J

Imari 14, 19, 20, 55
    English 54, 55
ironstone 52
Japanese influence 9, 28,
    30, 43, 64, 65, 66
Japanese taste 21
jasper 24
jasperware 53
Jingdezhen kilns 13

K, L

Kakiemon 19, 20, 28
Kändler, Johann Joachim
    30
kaolin 27, 49, 58, 59,
    66
Knight, Dame Laura 76
Laub- und Bandelwerk
    26, 29
Liverpool 22, 47, 48
Louis XV 32

M, N

maiolica 67
Majolica 67
Maria Theresa, Empress
    62

Meissen 8, 15, 25, 26, 27, 28, 29, 30, 31, 42
Minton 67
molding 36, 38, 42

N, O

Naples factory 63
Neoclassical style 35, 58, 63, 67
Newhall 54, 57
Oriental influence 67, 73
Osterspey, Jacob 35

P

parian 66
Paris porcelain 59
patterns 57, 74
political wares 70, 71
porcelain
    Chinese 8, 9, 14, 15, 17, 18, 22, 25
    hard-paste 13, 25, 27, 58, 59
    Japanese 9, 14, 43
    soft-paste 33, 41, 43, 48, 49, 58
    Vienna-style 62

R

Rhead, Frederick 70
Rhodes, David 45

rice-paper paintings 6, 10
Rococo style 42, 58
Rouen 33
Royal porcelain 58
Royal Vienna factory 62
Rozenburg factory 65

S

Sadler, John and Green, Guy 47
St. Cloud 33
Satsuma wares 21
Sèvres 15, 32, 33, 34, 58, 59
Shao Xuamao 16
Shelley Potteries 70
Shorter, Colley 74
silver teapots 15, 17, 23, 24, 25, 26, 31, 37, 38
Spode, Josiah 52, 57
stoneware 23, 24, 39, 40, 45, 50, 53
strapwork 23

T

teapot shapes
    Belleek 66
    camel 39, 73
    clown 76

Donald Duck 72
elephant 73
Empire 54
globular 12, 15, 17, 38
leaf molded 42
London 55, 57
phoenix 12
pineapple 44
rooster and hen 30
shell 37
transfer printing 46, 47, 52
Turner, John 51, 52, 53

V, W, Y

Versailles 32
Vezzi factory 27
Vincennes 32, 33
Wadeheath 72
Wedgwood, Josiah 44, 45, 46, 47, 50, 53
Wedgwood factory 51, 52, 75
Whieldon, Thomas 38, 45
Wilkinson's, A.J. 74, 76
Worcester 48, 49, 64
Yixing wares 12, 16, 24, 36

Acknowledgments

All pictures courtesy of Christie's South Kensington
except for the following:
Christie's Images: 7–8; 13–16t; 18–20; 22t; 23t; 24–28t;
29–42; 44–47; 49b; 51–54t; 58–59; 62; 64.
Clive Corless/Marshall Editions: 54b–55t; 56–57; 66b–67.
National Trust Photographic Library/John Bethell: 22b; 23b.
Illustrators: **Lorraine Harrison** (borders), **Debbie Hinks** (endpapers).